Published in the United States by Random House Children's Books,
a division of Random House, Inc., New York.

BEGINNER BOOKS, RANDOM HOUSE, and the Random House colophon are
registered trademarks of Random House, Inc. THE CAT IN THE HAT logo ® and
© Dr. Seuss Enterprises, L.P. 1957, renewed 1986. All rights reserved.

www.randomhouse.com/kids

Educators and librarians, for a variety of teaching tools, visit us at
www.randomhouse.com/teachers

Library of Congress Cataloging-in-Publication Data
Harris, Joe. The belly book / [written and illustrated] by Joe Harris. — 1st ed.   p. cm.
SUMMARY: Bellies can be used for many things, such as dancing the hula and resting your cup,
but it is important to feed them healthy foods, too.
ISBN 978-0-375-84340-2 (trade) — ISBN 978-0-375-94340-9 (lib. bdg.)
[1. Stomach—Fiction. 2. Stories in rhyme.] I. Title.   PZ8.3.H2426Be 2008   [E]—dc22   2006016630

Printed in the United States of America   10 9 8 7 6 5   First Edition

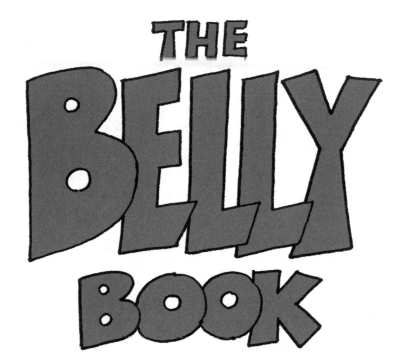

THE BELLY BOOK

by Joe Harris

BEGINNER BOOKS®
A Division of Random House, Inc.

Everybody has a belly.

Babies have them.

So do pops.

So do firemen.

So do cops.

People who play
ball have them.

People shopping in
the mall have them.

A sumo's belly
is big and fat.

A ballerina's belly
is small and flat.

My mom had a big belly
when she carried me!

A kangaroo belly
can carry two or three!

A whale has a belly
so big and wide
that you could park
a truck inside!

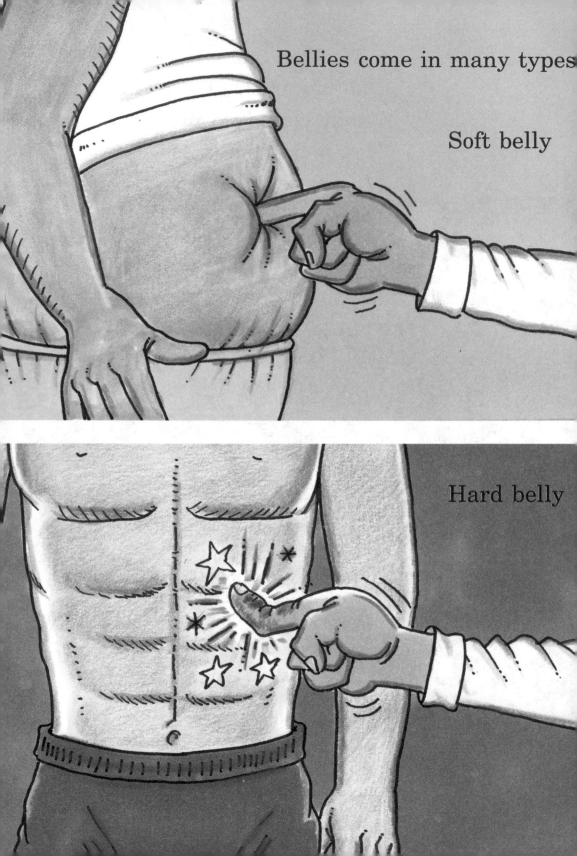

Bellies come in many types

Soft belly

Hard belly

Bunny belly

Funny belly

High belly

Low belly

Prickly belly

Sickly belly

Cold belly

Hot belly

Stinker belly

Tinkerbelly!

There are white bellies . . .

ight bellies . . .

green bellies . . .

clean bellies!

And did you know
there are glow bellies . . .

snow bellies . . .

brass bellies . . .   glass bellies?

And, down by the sea,
hula-dancing grass bellies?

A belly is great for
a number of things.
You can use it to help take
bags home from the store.

When your hands are full,
your belly can close the door.

A belly is great
for a nap on a plane

and for keeping cubs dry
when it's starting to rain.

A belly's a good place
for resting your cup.

It also works well
for a chat with your pup.

But bellies aren't great
when you can't read your weight

or get close enough
to hug your mate.

And a belly should never
get to the stage
when it can't even fit
on this double page.

To keep them from growling
and acting rude,
we should feed our bellies
lots of fresh, healthy food:

fruit and vegetables
and lots of whole grains,
milk for our bones,
and fish for our brains.

Here are a few
well-belly tips:

Go easy on junk food
like soda and chips.

Go easy on candy and
ice cream and cake . . .

. . . or you will end up
with a bad belly ache!

Take care of your belly.
And if you do,
your belly will take
good care of you!